JURASSIC PARK COLLECTIBLES

Kristof Thijs

First published 2018

Amberley Publishing
The Hill, Stroud
Gloucestershire, GL5 4EP

www.amberley-books.com

Copyright © Kristof Thijs, 2018

The right of Kristof Thijs to be identified as the Author of this work has been asserted in accordance with the Copyrights, Designs and Patents Act 1988.

ISBN 978 1 4456 7923 5 (print)
ISBN 978 1 4456 7924 2 (ebook)

All rights reserved. No part of this book may be reprinted or reproduced or utilised in any form or by any electronic, mechanical or other means, now known or hereafter invented, including photocopying and recording, or in any information storage or retrieval system, without the permission in writing from the Publishers.

British Library Cataloguing in Publication Data.
A catalogue record for this book is available from the British Library.

Origination by Amberley Publishing.
Printed in the UK.

Appointed GPSR EU Representative: Easy Access System Europe Oü, 16879218
Address: Mustamäe tee 50, 10621, Tallinn, Estonia
Contact Details: gpsr.requests@easproject.com, +358 40 500 3575

Contents

Foreword 4

Introduction 5

Collecting Jurassic Park 6

Chapter 1 Jurassic Park (1993) 7

Chapter 2 The Lost World: Jurassic Park (1997) 29

Chapter 3 Jurassic Park: Chaos Effect (1998) 49

Chapter 4 Jurassic Park III (2001) 56

Chapter 5 Closing the Gaps 72

Chapter 6 Jurassic World (2015) 80

Ancient Future 96

Acknowledgments 96

Foreword

When I was eleven years old I wandered though my local Belgian toy shop and stumbled upon a new line of dinosaur toys. I couldn't keep my eyes of them. The artwork with the glowing sunset, palm trees and the striking *Jurassic Park* logo made a big impression on me. Even though I didn't realise what these toys were about, I still got an Alan Grant figure. Later, I learned that a film was coming out about a theme park filled with dinosaurs, and that really got my attention. I got more and more toys, at first just for playing together with my other dinosaurs. I had some of the classics: Tyco's Smithsonian Institution line, the Carnegie Collection and all of the Laramie sets. After seeing the film, I jumped on the *Jurassic Park* bandwagon and got more and more items. All presents I got around that time involved *Jurassic Park*.

I quickly outgrew my playing phase and started treating these items as collectibles, keeping them in their original packages. The kids' playroom at my parents' home was transformed into a 'museum' where I displayed my collection of fossils, dinosaur models and *Jurassic Park* toys. I made entry tickets for my friends and family who came to visit and proudly showed them around. I loved telling stories about the fossils I found at the local marl quarry, but also about my finds at the local toy shop.

By the time I was fifteen years old I had gained so many items that my 'museum' had become too small, so I used my own bedroom for the museum, forcing myself to sleep in a room that was not much bigger than my bed. But it was all worth it. Now I was able to get large cardboard standees from the local cinema, shops and video store. My collection kept growing, and by the time I was sixteen I made my own website, www.jurassictoys.net. This allowed me to show off my collection to the rest of the world, and thanks to online auction sites I was able to get items that were never released in Europe.

Today I still have a room entirely dedicated to my collection. I have fond memories of every single item, and each has its own story. Holding them throws me back to the time when I was that little boy in the toy shop, staring at those amazing *Jurassic Park* toys.

With this book, I'm happy to take you back in time for a nostalgic throwback to 1993. Hold onto your butts for a toy story sixty-five million years in the making.

Introduction

Dinosaurs vanished from the earth over sixty-five million years ago. For centuries their remains have been wrongfully identified as mystical, god-like creatures. When Richard Owen branded these creatures as 'dinosauria' in 1842, the first instance of dinosaur mania broke loose. Life-size reproductions of prehistoric creatures based on nothing but a few bones were created for the Great Exhibition of 1854. Today these statues still reside in London's Crystal Palace Park.

Not long after Owen's publications, dozens of dinosaurs and prehistoric creatures were being discovered all over the world, and they soon took over the era's new medium: moving pictures. *Gertie the Dinosaur* in 1914, *The Lost World* in 1925 and *King Kong* in 1933 were just a few examples with extinct animals in starring roles. Along with these films came the first dinosaur merchandising. Louis Marx & Company were among the first companies to produce a complete line of toys inspired by dinosaurs from the silver screen. The toys proved to be so successful that other companies reproduced the exact same models. Although they were released in the 1950s, copies of these models show up in cheaper playsets today.

In the 1980s, dinosaurs continued to play a role in children's fantasy worlds. Companies like Safari LTD produced scientifically accurate models, while other companies like Tyco turned dinosaurs into war machines with their Dino-Riders line. The classic animated film *The Land Before Time* came out in 1989, which made sure children didn't forget about dinosaurs for another couple of years.

The biggest thing to happen to dinosaurs since Chicxulub was Steven Spielberg's *Jurassic Park* in 1993. It sparked the biggest example of dinosaur mania of all time. The film, based on Michael Crichton's novel, spawned not just four feature films; it was also the inspiration for a long-running toy line, several theme park rides, videogames, comic books series and a fan community that spares no expense.

Collecting Jurassic Park

Starting your own *Jurassic Park* collection is not hard. Over the course of twenty-five years, hundreds if not thousands of *Jurassic Park* toys, collectibles and merchandising of all sizes and price ranges have been produced. The easiest way to start collecting is by looking for toys on online auction sites and by visiting the local thrift shop. An official *Jurassic Park* or *Jurassic World* dinosaur can easily be recognised by the painted JP or JW mark. This mark was created by Universal Studios to differentiate the official merchandising from generic, widely available dinosaur toys.

Most *Jurassic Park* and *Jurassic World* toys can easily be bought online from auction sites such as eBay. Common items like the classic *Jurassic Park* toy line from 1993 aren't that expensive to buy, especially when they come loose. Some items, however, do sell for quite a lot of money. The Carnotaurus from 1994 can easily go for more than $500. Getting a big lot with lots of loose *Jurassic Park* dinosaurs and action figures might be the best way to start your collection. You can re-sell or trade items from the lot when your collection is expanding.

To get an indication of their value, it's worth to take a look on the JPtoys.com website. They have listed nearly every *Jurassic Park* toy ever released with an estimated value. Social media platforms like Facebook give you the opportunity to get in touch with other enthusiasts. Most fans are happy to help you get started and introduce you to the world of *Jurassic Park*. These social media platforms are also a good way to start or expand your collection by trading or buying directly from other fans.

The golden rule that applies to anyone who's starting any collection is to have fun! Buy what you like and display it however you enjoy it the most. Leave the toys in their original packaging or open them and let your kids play with them. It doesn't matter, as long as you're having a good time.

Chapter 1

Jurassic Park (1993)

Steven Spielberg's attempt to make a film based on Crichton's science fiction novel would not be an easy task. The book was written from a scientific point of view, which can be attributed to Crichton's background in medical studies. But with the help of screenwriter David Koepp, Crichton's own script drafts were rewritten. Violent scenes were omitted by making the film's tone family friendly. Scenes of vicious carnivores were balanced with those of gentle giants like Brachiosaurus and Triceratops. Crichton's lead characters, palaeontologist Alan Grant, palaeobotanist Ellie Sattler and mathematician Ian Malcolm, remained the leading characters in the film. Just like in the book, they were invited by billionaire John Hammond to inspect his island off the coast of Costa Rica. Dinosaurs, bioengineered by the InGen Corporation, were alive and breathing on Isla Nublar. When a rival company bribes the park's software engineer to steal dinosaur embryos, things go wrong, leading to the escape of the vicious carnivores, who wreak havoc in the park. The remaining Jurassic Park employees and visitors were forced to fight for their lives while waiting for their evacuation.

The film was a showcase of modern special effects. Stan Winston created state-of-the-art, life-sized dinosaur animatronics for all the close-up shots. Special effects artist Dennis Murren was asked to provide the full-body dinosaur shots by using stop-motion models. This classic special effect was made popular by stop-motion specialist Ray Harryhausen, who was responsible for the creature effects in dozens of films in the 1950s and '60s. When Steven Spielberg was shown a CGI demo of a hunting T-Rex, he abandoned the use of stop-motion completely. The realistic display and movement of the dinosaurs added to the success of the film.

Jurassic Park was a huge box office success. It was the highest grossing film ever, breaking the opening record set by *Batman Returns*. A wide assortment of toys, merchandising and collectibles also added to the financial success. To distinguish its merchandising from generic brands, a special JP mark was put on all *Jurassic Park* dinosaur toys. On top of that, the catchphrase 'If It's Not *Jurassic Park*, It's Extinct' was printed on almost all of the *Jurassic Park* merchandise packaging.

Kenner Toys

The *Jurassic Park* brand's most loyal licensee holder was Kenner, a well-established toy brand that operated under the Hasbro umbrella. It produced some iconic toy lines like M.A.S.K., The Real *Ghostbusters*, *The Terminator* and all the classic *Star Wars* toys. The first Kenner series of *Jurassic Park* toys was made up of five human action figures, eleven dinosaurs, three vehicles and a large playset.

It's not uncommon for companies to produce products based on early concepts of a film, and Kenner was no exception. This resulted in several action figures that bared almost no resemblance to the film's actors. This was corrected in the second series, one year later. Kenner also selected the characters they figured would be popular among children. There were no toy versions of characters like John Hammond, Ray Arnold, Doctor Wu and Lex Murphy. Ian Malcolm, probably one of the most popular *Jurassic Park* characters ever, was released later as part of Kenner's series II line.

Each human figure came with a weapon or accessory, a dinosaur hatchling and a collector's card designed by dinosaur artist Brian Franczak. All toys, except for the vehicles, came with such a collector's card.

The real stars of *Jurassic Park* were obviously the dinosaurs. There were five small dinosaurs and prehistoric creatures, each with a specific action. The Velociraptor and Dimetrodon had snapping jaws, the Dilophosaurus could spit water, the Pteranodon had flapping wings and the Coelophysis pair had bendable necks and tails.

The Electronic Velociraptor and Electronic Dilophosaurus could both produce a sound effect. It was branded by Kenner as 'Dino Screams in Electronic Sound'. The effect could be triggered by pulling the Velociraptor's legs backwards and by pushing the Dilophosaurus' arm down.

Jurassic Park action figures: Robert Muldoon, Alan Grant, Dennis Nedry, Ellie Sattler and Tim Murphy.

Jurassic Park dinosaurs: Dimetrodon, Velociraptor, Coelophysis, Pteranodon, Dilophosaurus.

Jurassic Park electronic dinosaurs: Velociraptor and Dilophosaurus.

Two dinosaurs that appeared in Crichton's book, but not in the film, were designed and released by Kenner. Spielberg swapped the Stegosaurus for a Triceratops in the film, and the Young Tyrannosaurus Rex from the book was not used in the film at all. Both toys had a soft rubbery skin and a Dino-Damage wound with a loose skin piece.

The Triceratops was one of the largest dinosaur in this toy line and was very popular when it was released. The Triceratops' head moved up and down by squeezing its side. Just like the Stegosaurus and Young Tyrannosaurus Rex, it had soft skin and a Dino-Damage wound.

The largest dinosaur in Kenner's first *Jurassic Park* series was the Electronic Tyrannosaurus Rex. An electronic growling sound and moving jaws could be activated by squeezing its torso. By putting its feet down on a surface, a stomping sound could be heard. The Electronic Tyrannosaurus Rex was a very popular toy, making it easy to find it at a good price.

Jurassic Park Stegosaurus.

Jurassic Park Young Tyrannosaurus Rex.

Jurassic Park Triceratops.

Jurassic Park Electronic Tyrannosaurus Rex.

Kenner produced two iconic *Jurassic Park* vehicles, which were directly inspired by the film. The Bush Devil Tracker resembled the Jeep Wrangler gas vehicle. It came with a snare, a missile launcher and a Dino-Damage windshield. The Jungle Explorer was based on the Ford Explorer tour vehicles. The hood could be removed as if it were ripped off by a dinosaur. It could also shoot missiles that would 'fill up with dinosaur blood'. However, the Capture Copter was not directly inspired by the helicopter seen in the film. It was equipped with a rocket launcher and a net that could be dropped by pushing a button.

The biggest *Jurassic Park* toy in this line was the Command Compound. It wasn't uncommon for toy companies in the 1980s and early '90s to produce large toy sets like this. Kenner's Ewok Village, Mattel's Grey Skull Castle and Hasbro's G.I. Joe USS *Flagg* captured the imaginations of boys and girls alike. The Command Compound was no

Jurassic Park (1993)

Jurassic Park Bush Devil Tracker and Jungle Explorer.

Jurassic Park Capture Copter.

Jurassic Park Electronic Command Compound.

Jurassic Park metal die-cast dinosaurs.

exception and it was probably one of Kenner's last big sets; *Jurassic Park* playsets that were produced for later lines got smaller and more compact every time.

The Command Compound came with the iconic *Jurassic Park* gate, fences and several break-away Dino-Damage pieces on its exterior. The interior featured a hatchery with hatching eggs, and an electronic computer that could speak over 100 phrases and sound an alarm when a fence was removed from the building.

Besides its action figures and big dinosaurs, Kenner also released six pairs of metal die-cast dinosaur statues. They had no playability and were produced solely from a collector's point of view. Each dinosaur came with its own collector's card with dinosaur facts and figures.

Kenner Series II

A sequel to the first toy line was released by Kenner in 1994. Twelve action figures, eleven dinosaurs and three vehicles were added to their prehistoric portfolio. Alongside new versions of the film's characters, a line of toys with a poaching subplot was released as well, which was not directly inspired by the happenings in the film. Several toys were announced in catalogues or on the packaging of the other toys, but were not produced at that time. Some were later released as part of the *The Lost World: Jurassic Park* line.

Characters from the film were re-released by Kenner in the series II line, but this time with new head sculpts and paint jobs. They also came with a different dinosaur hatchling and a new collector's card. Only the Ian Malcolm figure was a completely new action figure – all others had already appeared in the first toy line.

Jurassic Park series II Alan Grant, Ellie Sattler, Tim Murphy.

Jurassic Park series II Alan Grant and Dennis Nedry.

Jurassic Park series II Ian Malcolm and Robert Muldoon.

Jurassic Park series II Dino Trackers Sergeant T-Rex Turner, Jaws Jackson and Harpoon Harrisson; and Evil Raiders Dr Snare and Skinner.

Jurassic Park series II Pachycephalosaurus, Tanystropheus and Lycaenops.

The Dino Trackers and Evil Raiders (or Dino Raiders in some countries) were all new sculpts. Just like the film-based characters, they came with weapons, a dinosaur hatchling and a collector's card. A sixth action figure was announced but never released. Scrap Davis would have featured a robotic arm and a Dimetrodon hatchling.

Five small dinosaurs were part of the series II line. Pachycephalosaurus, Tanystropheus and Lycaenops were all brand-new sculpts. The Velociraptor and Dilophosaurus from the first series were re-issued, but this time with capture gear and a new collector's card. Three other prehistoric creatures were supposed to be part of this line: Estemennosuchus, Scutosaurus and Ornithosuchus. They weren't released until 1997, when *The Lost World: Jurassic Park* came out.

Only seven dinosaurs appeared in the *Jurassic Park* film and Gallimimus was one of them. Kenner waited until 1994 to release a toy version. The Electronic Gallimimus' legs kicked and produced a shrieking sound by pushing the button on its back. Baryonyx was also an electronic dinosaur in this line. Besides a sound effect, its jaws snapped when the right leg was pulled backwards. The Electronic Velociraptor and Dilophosaurus were re-released with a new collector's card.

Two mid-sized dinosaurs with soft skin were part of the series II toy line. The Young Tyrannosaurus Rex was a repaint from the first series, its tan colour replaced by gloomy black and green. It came with a new collector's card and with capture gear. A completely new dinosaur was the Carnotaurus. It had a striking, aggressive pose. Its sharp-looking claws and teeth revealed why it was nicknamed 'Demon'. The Carnotaurus is probably one of the most popular and sought after *Jurassic Park* toys of all time, making it very expensive to purchase.

Jurassic Park series II Gallimimus.

Jurassic Park series II Baryonyx.

Jurassic Park series II Young Tyrannosaurus Rex, displayed without capture gear.

Jurassic Park series II Carnotaurus, displayed without capture gear.

Instead of going for the typical Pteranodon or Pterodactyl, Kenner opted for the lesser-known Quetzalcoatlus. It was one of the largest flying creatures in the Late Cretaceous era. Kenner's version came in an enclosed box with artwork depicting the creature holding Dr Snare in its claws. The Quetzalcoatlus' wings flapped by pushing the button on its back. It came with capture gear.

Jurassic Park has often been criticised for the depiction of the Velociraptors. In the film they were as tall as an adult human, while in reality they weren't taller than 50 centimetres. However, in 1993 the remains of an until-then unknown carnivore were identified as Utahraptor. It was a menacing predator roughly the size of an adult human, just like the raptors in the film. Kenner used this opportunity to produce a toy based on this brand-new dinosaur. The Utahraptor was painted in a leopard-like colour scheme. It featured electronic growls and came with capture gear.

Three vehicles were designed as part of the Dino Trackers/Evil Raiders storyline. The Evil Raiders Strike Cycle was a motorcycle that featured a firing capture claw while the Dino Tracker Jungle Runner could fire a grappling hook. Repainted versions of the Bush Devil Tracker and Jungle Explorer were announced but never released.

The Capture Cruiser was the largest vehicle in the series II toy line. A large overhead strike net could be activated by pulling a handle on the front of the cruiser. The big net was secured on two pivoting arms by thin plastic pins that broke easily, making it almost impossible to find a used Capture Cruiser in mint condition. The vehicle was later re-released as part of Kenner's toy line inspired by the film *Congo*.

Jurassic Park series II Quetzalcoatlus, displayed without capture gear.

Jurassic Park series II Electronic Utahraptor.

Jurassic Park series II Dino Trackers Jungle Runner and Dino Raiders Strike Cycle.

Jurassic Park series II Capture Cruiser.

Other *Jurassic Park* Toys

Dakin was a toy brand that had produced stuffed animals since 1966. For the release of *Jurassic Park* they created two different lines of stuffed dinosaurs. One line featured rather cartoony designs, while the other line was much more inspired by the concept designs by ILM's Mark 'Crash' McCreery. This line featured four dinosaurs: Dilophosaurus, Triceratops, Velociraptor and Brachiosaurus, which to this day is still one of the biggest *Jurassic Park* toys ever produced. It stands over 31 inches or 80 centimetres tall, easily dwarfing the Alan Grant action figure.

Byggis was a LEGO-clone brand that produced a limited amount of brick sets in the early nineties. For *Jurassic Park* they released two large sets and several small add-on sets. Unlike LEGO, the Byggis sets combined plastic bricks with cardboard cutouts for the mini-figures and dinosaur heads.

Hasbro's Milton Bradley (MB) released several *Jurassic Park* products including puzzles and the *Jurassic Park* board game. This came with a large oversized board, Velociraptors and T-Rex figures and a cardboard Visitor Center. Players had to find their way through the park while escaping the dinosaurs by using the playcards. The board game was released using the Parker Brothers brand in some countries.

Jurassic Park Dilophosaurus, Velociraptor and Triceratops by Dakin.

Byggis *Jurassic Park* Dino World.

Left: Jurassic Park Brachiosaurus by Dakin, which is shown here with an Alan Grant action figure for height comparison.

Below: Jurassic Park board game by Parker Brothers.

Media

The early 1990s saw the uprising of videogames on all kinds of platforms. Ocean Software made *Jurassic Park* games for the Nintendo Entertainment System (NES), Super Nintendo, Game Boy and for PC. Sega developed its own game for their systems that were popular at the time. Hi Tech Entertainment released the *Jurassic Park: Paint and Activity Center*. With this software, the user could paint *Jurassic Park*-themed colouring pages, read storybooks and play mini-games, like a Pong clone.

Tiger Electronics gained fame in the late 1980s and early 1990s with their version of computer games. They produced several licensed handheld games like *Robocop*, *Teenage Mutant Ninja Turtles* and *Batman*. In their *Jurassic Park* game, the user played as Tim and Lex, who had to dodge attacking Velociraptors, spitting Dilophosaurus and the rampaging Tyrannosaurus Rex, all with the help of Dr Alan Grant.

For the VHS release, Universal Studios came up with a gift set in the shape of a DNA carry case. Besides the *Jurassic Park* VHS (or the *Making of Jurassic Park* in some countries), it came with a book about dinosaurs and their DNA. Also included were an InGen security pass, a 3D hologram watch and a map of Isla Nublar.

Jurassic Park videogames by Ocean Software and *Jurassic Park* Activity Center by Hi Tech Entertainment.

Jurassic Park handheld game by Tiger Electronics.

Jurassic Park DNA case.

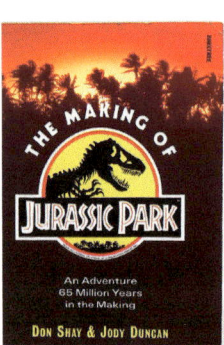

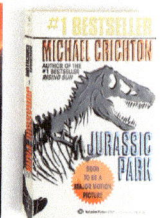

Various *Jurassic Park* books.

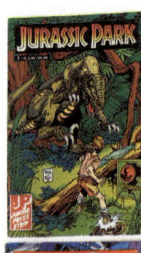

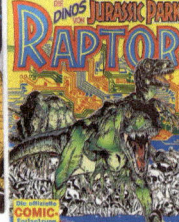
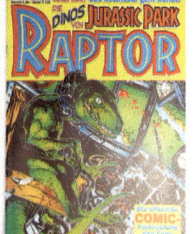

Jurassic Park comic books: Dutch and German variations.

The *Jurassic Park* film inspired several book releases, from junior novelisations to photo books. An interesting book that sheds light behind the scenes during the film's production was written by Don Shay and Jody Duncan. This making-of book is filled with dozens of rare behind the scenes photos and stories. It also exhibits several pieces of previsualisation art and concept drawings of scenes that did not make it in the film. One of those interesting pieces of art is that of the baby Triceratops. Lex was supposed to ride on its back at some point in the film. The scene was eventually removed from the script, even though a life-size model had already been built by Stan Winston Studios. An early version of the dust cover of this book was used as a movie prop in the *Jurassic Park* gift shop. It can be seen in the 'Remembering Petticoat Lane' scene.

Topps Comics published the official *Jurassic Park* comic book series between 1993 and 1997. The first four issues were a retelling of the film's storyline with art by veteran illustrators Gil Kane and George Pérez. The series ran for four years and totalled several chapters: 'Raptors', 'Raptors Attack', 'Raptors Hijack' and 'Return to Jurassic Park'. Topps also published a No. 0 issue that explored the story behind the construction of the park. Although these stories were inspired by the *Jurassic Park* novel and film, they are not considered to exist in the *Jurassic Park* Cinematic Universe. In 2010 IDW Publishing re-published all these *Jurassic Park* comic books in four *Classic Jurassic Park* volumes.

French publisher Ronde du Tournesol released several cut-out activity books inspired by *Jurassic Park* and its dinosaurs. One of those books was a recreation of Jurassic Park on Isla Nublar.

Jurassic Park activity books by Ronde du Tournesol.

Assorted *Jurassic Park* Collectibles

Above: *Jurassic Park*-inspired bedroom.

Left: *Jurassic Park* socks.

Above: *Jurassic Park* stationary by Copywrite.

Right: *Jurassic Park* desk chair.

Above: Assorted *Jurassic Park* wishing cards.

Left: Packaging of *Jurassic Park* crisps by Smiths.

Jurassic Park (1993)

Jurassic Park drinking glasses.

Jurassic Park View-Master set.

Jurassic Park SkyCaps.

Above: *Jurassic Park* video store shelf danglers.

Left: *Jurassic Park* cardboard standee.

Chapter 2

The Lost World: Jurassic Park (1997)

Following the success of *Jurassic Park*, Michael Crichton penned a sequel to his hit 1990 novel. This time the dinosaurs were roaming on Isla Sorna without enclosures or human interference for years. He named his novel *The Lost World* after Sir Arthur Conan Doyle's similar story about a remote island with a thriving dinosaur population.

After the novel was released in 1995, production on the film began by Universal Pictures. David Koepp wrote the screenplay, loosely based on the novel. A number of characters that Crichton created were heavily altered or completely left out: Jack Thorne, Richard Levine and Lewis Dogson never made it to Isla Sorna, while dinosaurs like Carnotaurus and Maiasaura remained extinct. Steven Spielberg returned to direct the film and Jeff Goldblum reprised his role as chaotician Ian Malcolm. He journeyed with a specialist team to Isla Sorna to join Sarah Harding, an animal behaviour specialist. She was asked by John Hammond to observe and document the dinosaurs' habits. The greedy InGen company, led by Hammond's nephew Peter Ludlow, also went to the island to capture live dinosaurs for their new *Jurassic Park* in San Diego. When the situation got out of hand, both the environmentalists and the hunters had to work together to get safely off the island.

The Lost World: Jurassic Park broke every box office opening record when it was released on 23 May 1997 in the United States. It was nominated for an Academy Award for best special effects, but lost to another box office giant – *Titanic*.

Kenner Toys

Kenner returned as the main toy manufacturer. Action figures, dinosaurs and vehicles were all designed in the same style as the first *Jurassic Park* toy line, but just like in 1993 the action figures were based on early script drafts. Some figures, like Eddie Carr and Nick Van Owen, had no resemblance to the film's actors. All action figures came with a weapon and a dinosaur hatchling. Unlike in 1993, there were no collector's cards included with any of the toys. Two versions of the Nick Van Owen figure exist: with and without baseball cap.

Six small dinosaurs – three repaints and three completely new sculpts – were released, each coming with capture gear. A new Velociraptor sculpt was introduced by Kenner that was not inspired by the film's version. The raptor was nicknamed 'Cyclops', referring to its one blind eye.

Four mid-sized electronic dinosaurs were part of this toy line. Each dinosaur had a specific action besides their sound effects. The Velociraptor had snapping jaws and

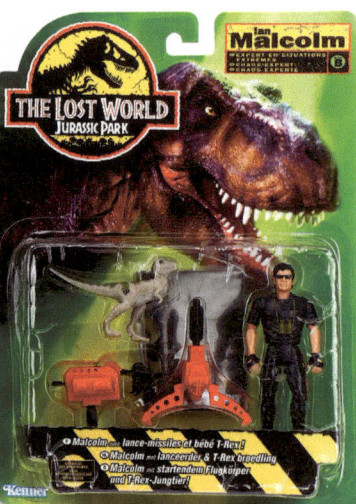

Above: *The Lost World: Jurassic Park* action figures: Eddie Carr, Roland Tembo and Nick Van Owen.

Left: *The Lost World: Jurassic Park* action figures: Dieter Stark and Ian Malcolm.

The Lost World: Jurassic Park action figures: Sarah Harding and Peter Ludlow.

The Lost World: Jurassic Park Velociraptor, Junior T-Rex, Dilophosaurus, Triceratops, Pachycephalosaurus, and Cyclops Velociraptor. All are shown without their capture gear.

the Parasaurolophus had kicking legs, while the Spinosaurus' mouth could open and close. Chasmosaurus, which was misspelled as 'Chasmasaurus', could move its head up and down.

The Stegosaurus, Pachycephalosaurus and Carnotaurus were part of the Dino-Strike subline. Each of these dinosaurs came with capture gear that the dinosaur could break free from with their own specific action. The Stegosaurus had a swinging tail and the Pachycephalosaurus could butt its head. Their bodies also had a Dino-Damage wound that could be covered up with a loose skin piece, just like the big dinosaurs from 1993.

The Carnotaurus in this toy line looked very different compared to the one from the *Jurassic Park* series II line. It was a completely new sculpt and was much bulkier compared to the 1994 version. Although there were no Carnotaurus in the movie, they played an important role in Michael Crichton's *The Lost World* novel.

A battle-ravaged Allosaurus was part of the Dino-Damage Medical Center. The dinosaur had several removable body parts and it could be tied down on the lab table, which was surrounded by all kinds of medical equipment.

The Lost World: Jurassic Park Electronic Chasmasaurus and Spinosaurus.

The Lost World: Jurassic Park Electronic Velociraptor and Parasaurolophus.

The Lost World: Jurassic Park Dino-Strike Pachycephalosaurus and Stegosaurus.

The Lost World: Jurassic Park Dino-Strike Carnotaurus, displayed without capture gear.

    Pteranodon made a small cameo at the end of the film. Kenner made a toy version that was based on the sculpt of the Quetzalcoatlus from 1994. Its wings could be locked in its sides, and by pushing the button on the back they would stretch out and flap.

Right: *The Lost World: Jurassic Park* Allosaurus from the Dino-Damage Medical Center set.

Below: *The Lost World: Jurassic Park* Pteranodon.

The Dino Tracker set featured two prehistoric animals that were originally planned for the 1994 *Jurassic Park* toy line: Estemennnosuchus and Scutosaurus. Both had Dino-Damage wounds and came with an action figure, capture gear and weapons. The Dino Tracker set was available exclusively at Toys 'R Us.

The Utahraptor from the *Jurassic Park* series II toy line was re-issued with a Dino-Tracker action figure and capture gear. It was also a Toys 'R Us exclusive. Another Toys 'R Us set was a re-issue of the Young Tyrannosaurus Rex with Dino Tracker.

The Thrasher T-Rex remains a popular collectible today. It featured a whole new sculpt, but was similar in size to the Red T-Rex from Kenner's first *Jurassic Park* toy line. By swinging its tail left and right, the head would move. The Thrasher T-Rex came with large pieces of capture gear. When worn, the T-Rex could break free from it by using the thrashing motion.

The Bull T-Rex, or the 'buck', as Roland Tembo referred to it in the film, was Kenner's biggest dinosaur. It was originally planned to be released in 1994 as part of the *Jurassic Park* series II line. The Bull T-Rex came with a safety pod holding a scared Jurassic Park employee. The pod could be pushed down the throat and retrieved

The Lost World: Jurassic Park Dino-Tracker Adventure Set.

The Lost World: Jurassic Park Utahraptor.

The Lost World: Jurassic Park Thrasher T-Rex, shown without capture gear.

through an opening in its stomach. The same sculpt was re-used two times: for the Chaos Effect line in 1998 and for the Toys 'R Us exclusive line in 2009.

There were four small playsets, each coming with an action figure inspired by a character from the film. The Glider Pack with Ian Malcolm was inspired by a scene that was cut from David Koepp's screenplay. It was supposed to take place during the scene with the Velociraptors in the Site B village. The survivors of the attack would have used gliders to escape the chaos, but would then be attacked by Pteranodons.

The Dino-Snare Dirtbike came with Carter, an InGen hunter who was seen briefly in the film. The Dirtbike came with a snare and could break apart by pushing the button on the back.

The High Hide was the cage-like contraption that Eddie Carr and Kelly Malcolm used to escape the attacking Tyrannosaurus Rex family. The toy version came with a Nick Van Owen figure.

The D.A.R.T., or Dino Auto Restraint Transport, was a trike that came with Roland Tembo, the only action figure in this line with bendable knees.

The Lost World: Jurassic Park Bull T-Rex.

The Lost World: Jurassic Park Glider Pack and Dino-Snare Dirtbike.

Above: *The Lost World: Jurassic Park* D.A.R.T. and High Hide.

Left: *The Lost World: Jurassic Park* Net Trapper and Ground Tracker.

    The Net Trapper and Ground Tracker were loosely inspired by the on-screen vehicles. The Ground Tracker came with battery-operated overhead lights and a Dino-Damage popping car hood. The Net Trapper had a big net on one side that could hold a small dinosaur, like a Velociraptor or Pachycephalosaurus.

    The Humvee was inspired by the InGen Hummer vehicle that was used in the herd chasing scene. Just like in the film, a large dinosaur contraption device could be attached to the front of the vehicle. Two seats on each side of the Humvee could be pulled out and could hold action figures.

    The Mobile Command Center was a large playset based on the famous trailer from the film. The back side could open up to reveal a laboratory, the overhead lights were battery operated and produced sound effects, and an exclusive Kelly Malcolm action figure was included. She's the only Afro-American character from any *Jurassic Park* film who was made as a toy by Kenner and Hasbro, and is one of the very few female characters.

Three large *Jurassic Park* baby dinosaur hatchlings were also part of Kenner's line, coming in large eggshells. The Triceratops and Velociraptor were re-issues from 1993 but the Tyrannosaurus Rex hatchling was new and had a bandage on its leg, just like in the film.

The Lost World: Jurassic Park Humvee.

The Lost World: Jurassic Park Mobile Command Center.

The Lost World: Jurassic Park T-Rex, Velociraptor and Triceratops hatchlings.

Kenner Series II

A limited second series of toys was produced by Kenner. Only three action figures and two dinosaurs were part of this line. A Triceratops toy with a hunter's tent was announced but was never released. The Nick Van Owen series II action figure is very hard to find today, making it quite expensive to purchase.

The Lost World: Jurassic Park series II Eddie Carr and Ajay.

The Lost World: Jurassic Park series II Nick Van Owen and Brachiosaurus hatchling, displayed without weapons.

The Lost World: Jurassic Park series II Ornithosuchus and Baryonyx.

Other Toy Brands

Toymaker Tyco returned as a *Jurassic Park* licensee. They produced several electronic devices that tied in with the film. Their two flagship toys were the Radio Control Truck with a spitting Dilophosaurus and an Electric Race Set. The race set came with cardboard backdrops and a Tyrannosaurus Rex figure that lashed out at passing InGen trucks. Tyco also had a smaller race set in 1993 that was based on *Jurassic Park*.

Mattel's Matchbox produced the Site B Action System Playsets. The Garage and the Fuel Depot were inspired by the InGen village from the film. Both featured pop-up Velociraptors. Eight playpacks in the tradition of the classic Matchbox toy vehicles were also part of this line. The vehicles were loosely inspired by the film's vehicles and each came with one or more dinosaurs.

Hasbro's Milton Bradley once again produced the official board game. It was designed as a sequel to their *Jurassic Park* board game, and just like in 1993 it came with an oversized board, several dinosaur figures and cardboard buildings.

MicroVerse, another brand by Hasbro, made playsets inspired by key scenes from the film. Vehicle and dinosaur packs were sold separately as an add-on to these playsets.

The Lost World: Jurassic Park remote-control truck by Tyco.

The Lost World: Jurassic Park Electric Race Set by Tyco.

The Lost World: Jurassic Park Matchbox die-cast vehicles.

The Lost World: Jurassic Park board game by Milton Bradley.

The Lost World: Jurassic Park T-Rex Trap and *The Lost World* Lab micro playsets by Microverse.

Media

Videogames with 3D renderings were all the rage in the mid-nineties thanks to the release of game consoles like the Playstation. A *The Lost World: Jurassic Park* game was made by Dreamworks Interactive for the Playstation and Sega Saturn platforms. The game's soundtrack was composed by newcomer Michael Giacchino. He used a live orchestra for this soundtrack, which was something that hadn't been done before for a videogame. The game soundtrack was released on CD in 1998.

Chaos Island was another game developed by Dreamworks Interactive and was a strategy videogame. The user had to build a basecamp and defend it from attacking dinosaurs and InGen hunters.

A first person shooter game called *Trespasser* was also developed by Dreamworks Interactive and released by Electronic Arts. It was conceived as a sequel to the film and featured the voices of Richard Attenborough as John Hammond and actress Minnie Driver as Anne, the game's hero. Due to scheduling issues the game was released too early and many bugs and errors remained in the game. This led the game to receive only negative reviews. In the documentary *Atari: Game over*, *Trespasser* was mentioned as being the worst videogame of all time. The Trescom fan community has been making mods for the game since its release, creating their own patches that solved many of the game's glitches.

The John Williams soundtrack was released on CD by MCA in 1997, a few months before the film's theatrical release. The packaging was a 3D pop-out diorama with dinosaurs in a lush jungle setting.

The Lost World: Jurassic Park Trespasser, Playstation game and *Chaos Island.*

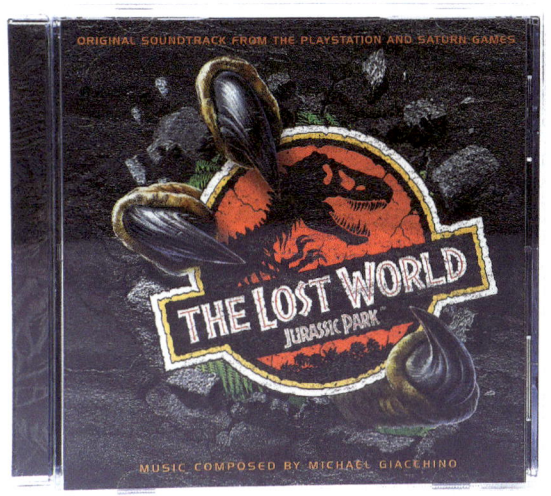

The Lost World: Jurassic Park game soundtrack by Michael Giacchino.

The Lost World: Jurassic Park soundtrack by John Williams.

A number of *The Lost World: Jurassic Park* books were released to accompany the film. Most of them were intended for younger readers, like the *Find Your Way to The Lost World Jurassic Park* paperback. The reader had to make choices while reading the book, which led to different endings. A book that catered to a more adult audience was *The Making of The Lost World: Jurassic Park*, written by Jody Duncan. It showcased the progress of how the film came to life with behind-the-scenes photos, as well as artwork and storyboards. Topps made a four-issue official film adaption. It would be the last series of *Jurassic Park* comic books until 2010.

Philips gave away a free *Behind the Scenes of The Lost World: Jurassic Park* with the purchase of their blank VHS tapes.

Above: Assorted *The Lost World: Jurassic Park* books.

Left: Behind the Scenes of *The Lost World: Jurassic Park* VHS by Philips. Cereal box toys by Nestlé.

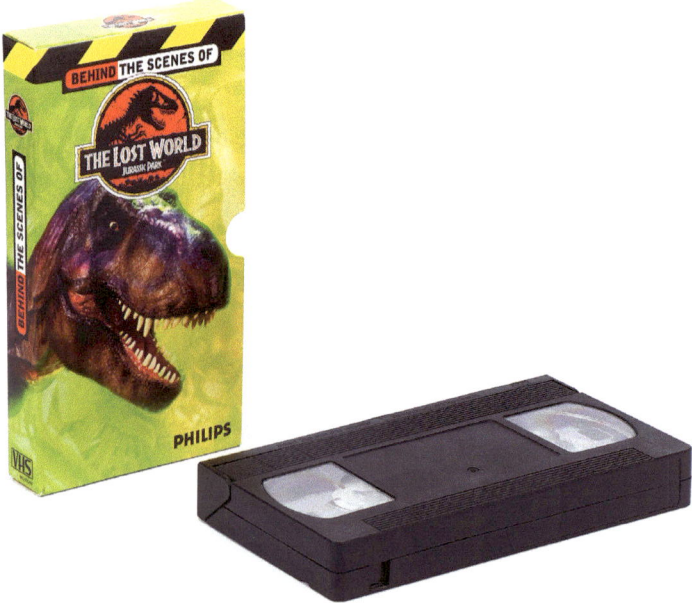

Assorted *The Lost World: Jurassic Park* Collectibles

  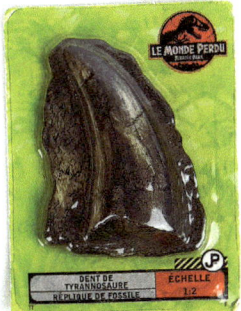 

  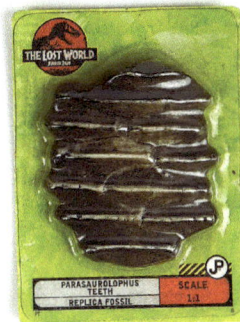 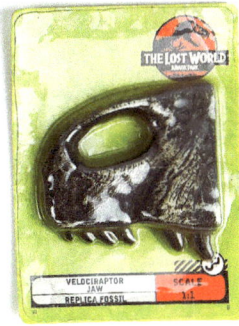

Each replica fossil was inspired by a dinosaur from *The Lost World: Jurassic Park*.

The Lost World: Jurassic Park milk chocolate eggs with surprise.

Above: Dinosaurus biscuits with *The Lost World: Jurassic Park* tattoo gift.

Left: *The Lost World: Jurassic Park* toothbrush holder.

Above left: Dixan washing powder with *The Lost World: Jurassic Park* branding.

Above right: *The Lost World: Jurassic Park* oversized cup with Velociraptor head.

Below: *The Lost World: Jurassic Park* drinking glasses.

Above: *The Lost World: Jurassic Park* puzzles by Milton Bradley.

Left: *The Lost World: Jurassic Park* theatre standee with motion-activated sound effects.

Chapter 3

Jurassic Park: Chaos Effect (1998)

Kenner produced the *Jurassic Park:* Chaos Effect line in 1998 following the success of *The Lost World: Jurassic Park*. This toy line sets itself apart from Kenner's previous dinosaur styles. Gone were the earth tones and detailed skin structure; instead they were smooth and had bright colours.

The origin of Chaos Effect traces back to a cancelled animated series that would have followed the adventures of Ian Malcolm and Roland Tembo on Isla Sorna. Dinosaurs had evolved into new, bizarre species following Ian Malcolm's chaos theory. Although the animated series was never produced, Kenner went ahead with the toy line anyway. They re-used sculpts from previous lines, now painted in bright new colours. They also came up with all new sculpts in a much different style. These new sculpts of hybrid dinosaurs were sleek and smooth, obviously mimicking the style of the animated series. Their names were usually a portmanteau, combining the names of other creatures. For example the name Velocirapteryx originated from Velociraptor and Archaeopteryx.

Over the years plenty of artwork for unreleased hybrids and figures emerged, like a brightly coloured Triceratops and Ankylosaurus. One Chaos Effect hybrid received a cult status among *Jurassic Park* fans: the Ultimasaurus. It was a combination of Triceratops, Velociraptor, Tyrannosaurus Rex, Stegosaurus and Ankylosaurus. Despite being featured in catalogues and box artwork, it was never released. A demo version was on display during the American International Toy Fair of 1998 and has since captured the imagination of many fans. Only a hatchling version of the Ultimasaurus was commercially available as part of the Roland Tembo action figure.

Jurassic Park: Chaos Effect Ultimasaurus hatchling.

Jurassic Park: Chaos Effect Raptor Alpha.

Jurassic Park: Chaos Effect Tanaconda.

Jurassic Park: Chaos Effect Amargospinus.

Ten hybrid dinosaurs were released, half of which were brand-new sculpts. The Omega T-Rex, Velociraptor, Tanaconda and Tyrannonops were repaints from other *Jurassic Park* toy lines. Besides their new paint scheme, there were no changes made to their sculpt. Compstegnathus, Amargospinus and Ankyloranodon were all brand-new designs.

Jurassic Park: Chaos Effect Tyrannonops.

Jurassic Park: Chaos Effect Compstegnathus.

Jurassic Park: Chaos Effect Ankyloranodon.

The mid-sized Electronic Velocirapteryx and Paradeinonychus were also new sculpts. They could produce a roaring sound effect. The head and arms of the Velocirapteryx moved by pulling its leg backwards. Pulling the Paradeinonychus' tail made it open its mouth and move its arms.

The Chaos Effect Thrasher T-Rex was a repainted version of the one released for *The Lost World: Jurassic Park*. Instead of the original's greyish paint scheme, the Chaos Effect version boasted striking yellow, blue and black colours. The head thrashing action, by shaking the tail left and right, remained the same. This time the T-Rex came without capture gear.

Jurassic Park: Chaos Effect Velociraptoryx.

Jurassic Park: Chaos Effect Paradeinonychus.

Another repaint from *The Lost World: Jurassic Park* was the Omega T-Rex. It was painted in bright orange and black. Just like in 1997, it came with an escape pod that could be swallowed by the T-Rex.

The Roland Tembo and Ian Malcolm action figures came with their own weapons and a hybrid hatchling. Their sculpts were completely new and different compared to the action figures from *The Lost World: Jurassic Park*.

Four vehicles were also part of this line, one of which was a repainted version of the Mobile Command Center from *The Lost World: Jurassic Park*. The Land and Air S.A.B.R.E. each came with an action figure. The Trike Dozer was a bulky vehicle with a large spring-loaded claw.

Jurassic Park: Chaos Effect Thrasher T-Rex.

Jurassic Park: Chaos Effect Omega T-Rex.

Jurassic Park: Chaos Effect Ian Malcolm and Roland Tembo.

Jurassic Park: Chaos Effect Land S.A.B.R.E.

Jurassic Park: Chaos Effect Air S.A.B.R.E.

Jurassic Park: Chaos Effect Trike Dozer.

Chapter 4

Jurassic Park III (2001)

Universal Studios began production on *Jurassic Park III* not long after *The Lost World: Jurassic Park* was released in theatres. Several script versions were pitched but every version got turned down by executive producer Steven Spielberg and director Joe Johnston. Two names were being tossed around during pre-production: *Jurassic Park: Extinction* and *Jurassic Park: Breakout*. The studio eventually settled for a version by Peter Buchman and named it simply *Jurassic Park III*. Shooting began with Sam Neill returning as Alan Grant, Téa Leoni, William H. Macy and Alessandro Nivola. While the production was fully up and running, changes were made to the script by bringing in screenwriters Alexander Payne and Jim Taylor. They reworked Buchman's script five weeks before shooting started.

In Payne and Taylor's version of *Jurassic Park III*, Alan Grant was tricked by a divorcing couple to go to Isla Sorna, the island featured in *The Lost World: Jurassic Park*. Their son, Eric, had gone missing after an accident with a parasailing boat, but when they arrived on the island, the rescue mission turned into a race against furious Velociraptors, vicious Pteranodons and the Spinosaurus, a new dinosaur in the *Jurassic Park* saga.

The dinosaurs came back to life once again thanks to ILM and Stan Winston Studios but this time they underwent some radical changes compared to the previous films. Quills were added to the Velociraptors' heads, Brachiosaurus were green opposed to grey as they were in *Jurassic Park* and the Pteranodons were of a completely new design to the ones from *The Lost World: Jurassic Park*.

Jurassic Park III received mostly negative reviews and received a Razzie for worst remake or sequel. Despite this, the film was considered a financial success.

Hasbro Toys

Hasbro produced the toy line for *Jurassic Park III*, this time using its own branding instead of Kenner's. The look and feel of the entire line was reinvented. Action figures were scaled down to 3.37 inches, compared to Kenner's 4.5 inches. Most dinosaurs were no longer in scale with the action figures. Instead, predators like Tyrannosaurus Rex, Spinosaurus and Velociraptor were all the same height. Only the large Animatronic Spinosaurus appeared to be in scale with the old-school Kenner dinosaurs.

All human action figures came with a miniature dinosaur and a weapon, none of which were spring loaded. Two unnamed military figures were released – a general and a diver – that were not directly inspired by the film's characters. They were most likely based on characters from an early draft of the screenplay.

Jurassic Park III action figures: Eric Kirby and Military General.

Jurassic Park III action figures: Amanda Kirby, Dr Alan Grant and Billy Brennan.

The sub-theme for the toy line was 'Re-Ak At-Ak'. The electronic dinosaurs would growl when a button was pushed on their Dino-Damage wound and when a leg or arm was pulled down. This time the Dino-Damage wound could not be covered up with a loose skin. There were ten small electronic dinosaurs, which were released in several waves. They came in open boxes, which made it easy to try out all the 'Re-Ak At-Ak' effects before buying them. The Dilophosaurus and Tapejara were the only dinosaurs in this line that didn't appear in the film.

Jurassic Park III second-wave action figures Dr Alan Grant, Paul Kirby and Military Diver.

Jurassic Park III dinosaurs: Triceratops, Pteranodon and Dilophosaurus.

Jurassic Park III dinosaurs: T-Rex, Alpha Velociraptor and Spinosaurus.

Jurassic Park III dinosaurs: Spinosaurus Aqua Attack and Tapejara.

Jurassic Park III dinosaurs: Brachiosaurus and Pack Raptor.

Jurassic Park III Alpha Pteranodon.

Jurassic Park III T-Rex.

Alpha Pteranodon was one of the larger toys. Its wings were too wide to fit the box, so they were made foldable, similar to the smaller Pteranodon that came with the Eric Kirby action figure. By pushing the button on its back, the Pteranodon made a sound effect and its wings would move up and down.

The sculpt of the large Tyrannosaurus Rex was considerably smaller than the old Kenner versions. This T-Rex produced sound effects by pushing the button in its wound and pulling its arm down. A stomping sound could be triggered by putting it down on a surface – an effect that the 1993 Kenner version also featured.

The Animatronic Spinosaurus was probably Hasbro's most ambitious *Jurassic Park* toy. An animated motion of its head and growling sounds could be triggered by pushing several buttons that were hidden under its soft latex skin. However, the mechanism was extremely vulnerable, so finding one in perfect condition is not that easy.

Above: *Jurassic Park III* Animatronic Spinosaurus.

Right: *Jurassic Park III* Stalking Raptor.

Hasbro didn't stop there with moving dinosaurs. Besides a remote control Spinosaurus, they released the interactive Stalking Raptor. By blowing on the Velociraptor skull, which was inspired by the resonating chamber in the film, it started walking and moving its head.

Hasbro released two posable dinosaurs: a Velociraptor and a Spinosaurus. Neither were really posable. They were actually made from a soft material that could bend, but would return to its original position when released.

There were three electric vehicles, each coming with an action figure. Neither of the vehicles were directly inspired by scenes from the film. The Raptor Motorcycle Pursuit came with an Alan Grant action figure and a Velociraptor, while the Air Heli-Sabre Marine Copter came with a pilot action figure.

The All-Terrain Dino Trapper was the biggest vehicle of this toy line. Somewhat similar to the Capture Cruiser from the *Jurassic Park* series II line, the ATDT could

Jurassic Park III Posable Velociraptor and Spinosaurus.

Jurassic Park III Air Heli-Sabre Marine Copter and Raptor Motorcycle Pursuit.

launch a net from the front of the truck, and its gun had flashing lights and sound effects. It came with a Billy Brennan action figure.

The Raptor Attack Playset was a re-issue of the *Jurassic Park* gate from the 1993 Command Compound set. It came with several fences, a net launcher and a rocket launcher. The Alan Grant figure and Velociraptor were repaints from the Raptor Motorcycle Pursuit set.

Jurassic Park III All-Terrain Dino Trapper.

Jurassic Park III Raptor Attack Playset.

Jurassic Park III CamoXtreme

A sequel to Hasbro's *Jurassic Park III* toy line received a limited release in 2002. It was dubbed 'CamoXtreme'. All dinosaurs were repaints from the 2001 toy line, but their designs were inspired by natural settings like the desert, Arctic and jungle. Only a limited amount of toys were produced and were sold in select online stores. In 2003, some of these toys showed up in discount stores across Europe.

The CamoXtreme two-packs were repaints of the miniature dinosaurs that came with the *Jurassic Park III* action figures. Just like in 1993, the two-packs came with a collector's card explaining the dinosaurs' camouflage. A few sample sets of the unreleased Jungle Spinosaurus and Tyrannosaurus showed up on eBay, selling at high prices.

Three mid-sized electronic 'Re-Ak At-Ak' dinosaurs were repainted, each with their own nature theme. The Tropical Velociraptor, Desert Spinosaurus and Lava Pteranodon were mentioned in Hasbro catalogues but were never commercially available. The Night Velociraptor is one of the rarest *Jurassic Park* toys today.

The Canyon T-Rex was the largest CamoXtreme dinosaur. Its colours resembled that of a milk snake. All the sound effects were the same as the Re-Ak At-Ak version from the year before.

Jurassic Park III CamoXtreme Arctic Spinosaurus/Stegosaurus and Lava T-Rex/Velociraptor

Jurassic Park III CamoXtreme Desert Spinosaurus/Velociraptor and Swamp Spinosaurus/T-Rex.

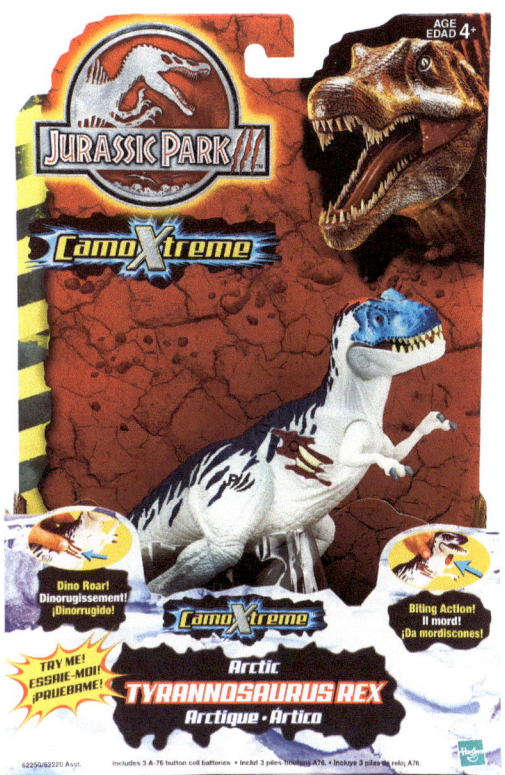

Jurassic Park III CamoXtreme Arctic Tyrannosaurus Rex.

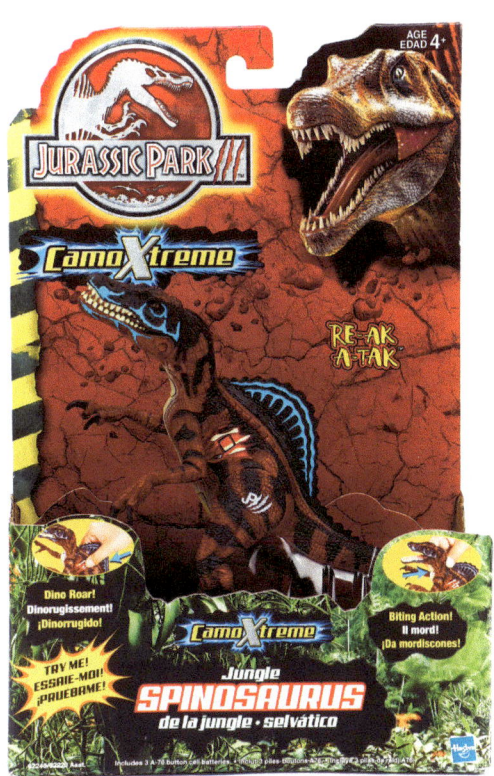

Jurassic Park III CamoXtreme Jungle Spinosaurus.

Left: Jurassic Park III CamoXtreme Night Velociraptor.

Below: Jurassic Park III CamoXtreme Canyon Tyrannosaurus Rex.

Other Toy Brands

Hasbro's Milton Bradley produced, for the third time, a *Jurassic Park* board game. The Island Survival Game came with a large game board and twelve dinosaurs. The players had to use their film character pawns to cross the island while escaping the dinosaurs.

Above: *Jurassic Park III* Island Survival Game by Milton Bradley.

Right: *Jurassic Park III* Dino Dex by Tiger Electronics.

Jurassic Park III electronic keychains by Tiger Electronics.

Jurassic Park III Spinosaurus Attack and Raptor Rumble by LEGO.

Hasbro's Tiger Electronics carried an assortment of electronic *Jurassic Park III* games and toys, like a set of electronic dinosaur keychains. The Dino Dex was inspired by the Pokédex from *Pokémon*. It had built-in information on seventy dinosaurs and two games: *Battle Dome* and the *DNA Lab*. The Dino Dex was also an organiser, coming with an address book and calculator.

LEGO acquired the *Jurassic Park* licence for the first time in 2001. Two *Jurassic Park III* sets were released as part of their LEGO Studios line, which was endorsed by Steven Spielberg. The sets were an add-on for the Moviemaker set that came with a real camera and stop-motion software. The dinosaurs used in these sets were not as polished as those that appeared in later LEGO sets.

Media

Scott Ciencin wrote the junior novelisation based on Peter Buchman's screenplay. He also wrote the *Jurassic Park Adventures* trilogy about Eric Kirby's time on Isla Sorna. The trilogy revealed some of the unexplained happenings from the film, like how Ben Hildebrand died.

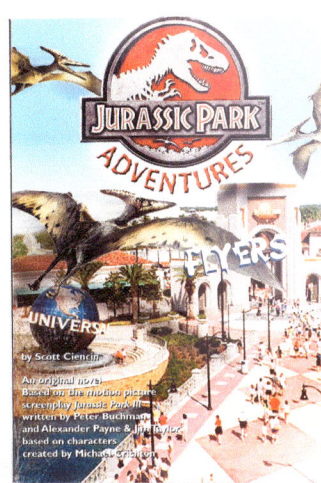

Above: Jurassic Park III books.

Right: Jurassic Park: Scan Command videogame by Knowledge Adventure.

Jurassic Park: Scan Command was a strategy videogame by Knowledge Adventure. The user was in control of a dinosaur and had to use it to stop the game's human villain. *Scan Command* came with a battery-operated scanning device. By scanning random barcodes, the user's dinosaur could be upgraded with better powers.

Assorted *Jurassic Park III* Collectibles

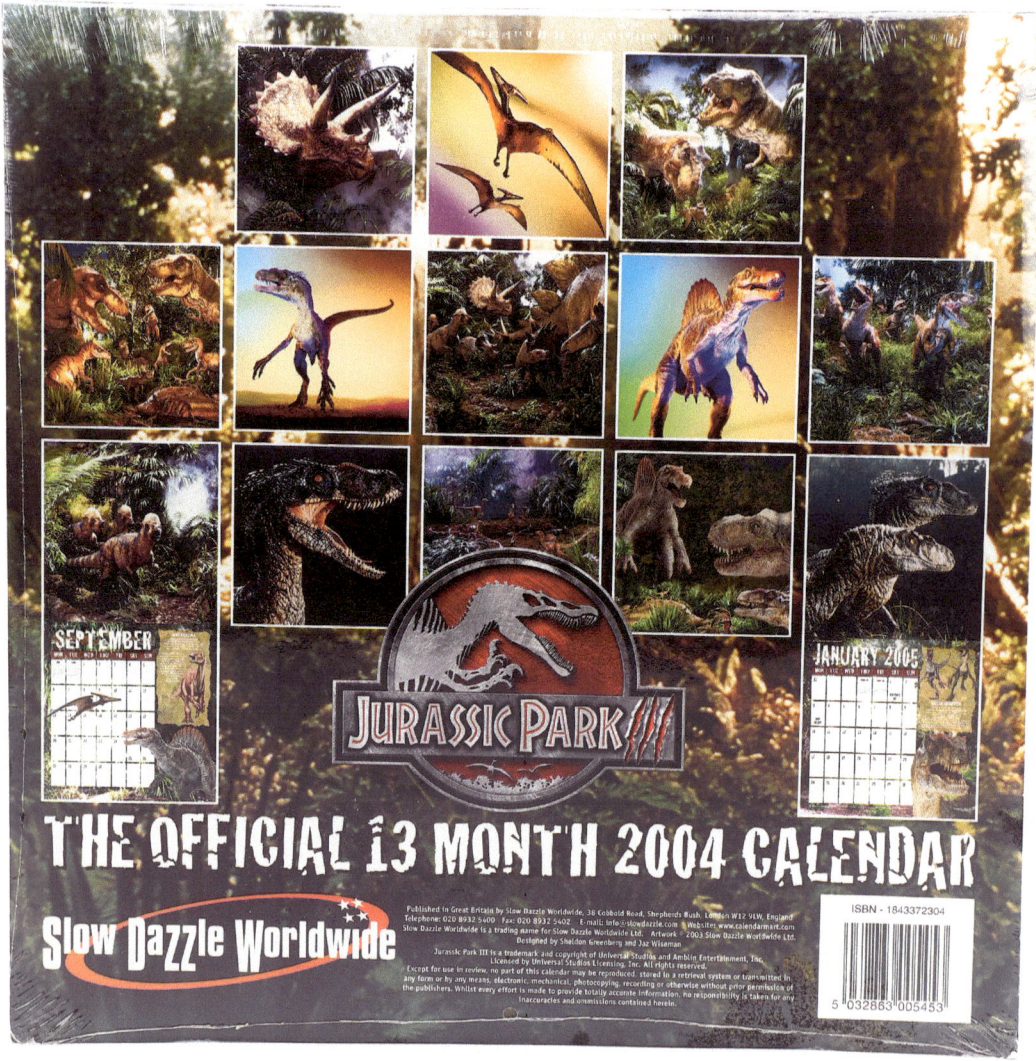

Jurassic Park III calendar by Slow Dazzle Worldwide.

Nestlé cereal boxes with *Jurassic Park III* lenticular cards.

Jurassic Park III hand puppets from Belgian fast food chain Quick.

Chapter 5

Closing the Gaps

Hasbro Toys

In 1999, Hasbro came up with its first line made entirely out of repainted *Jurassic Park* toys. The *Jurassic Park*: Dinosaurs line was only available at Wal-Mart and the Universal Studios theme parks. Both human figures and dinosaurs from the *Jurassic Park* and *The Lost World: Jurassic Park* toy lines were repurposed. The action figures were no longer based on characters from the films; instead, they were named in the likes of Dino Tracker, Dino Trainer, Dino Hunter and Dino Adventurer. Nineteen sets were released between 1999 and 2000.

In an effort to bring the *Jurassic Park* brand to a younger audience, Hasbro's Playskool cooked up a brand-new line for preschoolers in 2001. All dinosaurs and figures were designed to look friendly and playful. Eleven sets, from small single dinosaurs to big playsets, were produced for this Playskool line.

In 2004, two years after the release of the *Jurassic Park III:* CamoXtreme line, Hasbro brought its older sculpts back to life. The second *Jurassic Park:* Dinosaurs line was available exclusively at KB-Toys. There were four two-packs with repaints of the *Jurassic Park III* miniature dinosaurs. There were also four human/dinosaur packs; each had an action figure from the *Jurassic Park III* line and a dinosaur from the old Kenner lines. Finally, there were five electronic dinosaurs, all of which were repaints from the *Jurassic Park III* line.

A third *Jurassic Park:* Dinosaurs line hit the shelves a year later. There were nine sets, but this time with only sculpts from Hasbro's 2001 line. A new Triceratops sculpt was included in this line, which may have been an unreleased *Jurassic Park III* toy.

Jurassic Park: Dinosaurs Pteranodon and Young T-Rex.

Above: *Jurassic Park* Junior Double Trouble Dinos.

Right: *Jurassic Park* Junior Tracking the T-Rex.

Jurassic Park: Dinosaurs Brachiosaurus and Triceratops (2004).

Jurassic Park: Dinosaurs Triceratops with Dino Wrangler (2004).

In 2009, a new line of repaints was available at Toys 'R Us and the Universal Studios theme parks. All of the dinosaurs and action figures were repaints from the *Jurassic Park III* line, with the exception of the large Tyrannosaurus Rex, which was a slightly retooled version of the Bull Tyrannosaurus Rex from *The Lost World: Jurassic Park*.

Hasbro celebrated the 20th anniversary of *Jurassic Park* by releasing another toy line, this time called Dino Showdown. The entire line was a re-issue of the 2009 repaints, with the exception of two sets. These were completely new sculpts of an Allosaurus and a Pachyrhinosaurus. Each came with a new action figure, straight out of Hasbro's G.I. Joe vault. These new dinosaurs were highly articulated and had a Dino-Damage wound that could be covered up with a loose skin piece. A Stegosaurus was also supposed to be part of the Dino Showdown line but it never got released, despite being displayed on the packages.

Right: *Jurassic Park:* Dinosaurs Triceratops and Tyrannosaurus Rex (2005).

Below: *Jurassic Park:* Dinosaurs Tyrannosaurus Rex (2005).

Above: Jurassic Park 2009 line: Tyrannosaurus Rex, Velociraptor, Triceratops and Dilophosaurus.

Left: Jurassic Park Dino Showdown Pachyrhinosaurus Clash.

Jurassic Park Dino Showdown Allosaurus Assault.

Media

Several videogame companies released videogames over the years that were not directly tied to a film release:

Warpath: Jurassic Park came out in 1999 for Playstation. It was a single or multiplayer dinosaur fighting game. The arenas were settings from both *Jurassic Park* and *The Lost World: Jurassic Park,* like the Visitor Center from the first film and the 76 gas station from the San Diego rampage scene in the second film.

Jurassic Park: Operation Genesis was a 2003 theme park simulator for PC, Playstation 2 and Xbox. The user was able to build the park from scratch and hatch dinosaurs to inhabit it and attract visitors.

Telltale Games developed the four-part *Jurassic Park: The Game* for Playstation 3, Xbox 360, PC, Mac and iOS. It came out in 2011 and was based on side events that happened when the power went down on Isla Nublar. A PC version was released on DVD and came with a *Jurassic Park* souvenir map.

Universal Studios released all three *Jurassic Park* films for the first time on Blu-ray in 2013. For the occasion, a gift set with a statue of the Tyrannosaurus Rex breaking through the *Jurassic Park* gate was available for a limited time.

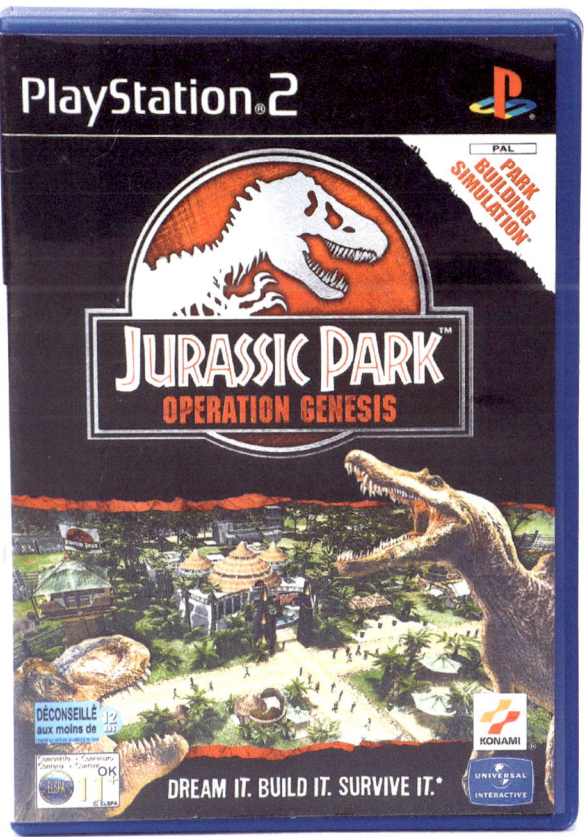

Jurassic Park: Operation Genesis for Playstation 2.

Warpath: Jurassic Park for Playstation.

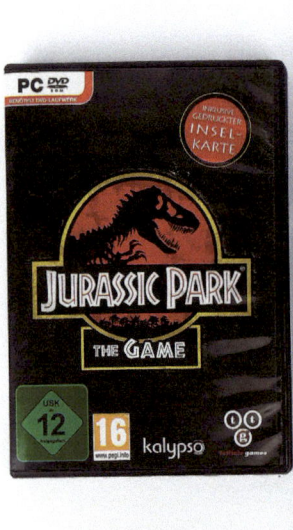

Jurassic Park: The Game for PC.

Jurassic Park Limited Edition Giftset.

Chapter 6

Jurassic World (2015)

Jurassic World marked the reboot of the *Jurassic Park* franchise. Universal Studios tried to move forward with a fourth film several times, but the project got stuck in production hell. Several script versions and revisions were being tossed around. The John Sayles draft involved trained hybrid dinosaurs that were used to save a kidnapped girl from a group of terrorists in Tangier. Eventually, Colin Trevorrow, director of the indie film *Safety Not Guaranteed,* was brought in. He rewrote the screenplay by Rick Jaffa and Amanda Silver, and some elements of the Sayles script were somewhat reused: a menacing hybrid dinosaur that could camouflage, trained Velociraptors and their human alpha.

Trevorrow and writing partner Derek Connelly stuck to Jaffa and Silver's concept of a Jurassic theme park in operation where things go wrong. They made sure many nods to the original film were incorporated, like the ruins of the original Jurassic Park visitor centre, the *Jurassic Park* Jeep Wranglers and the original Tyrannosaurus Rex. Only one character from the previous films was brought back: Dr Wu. He was now the leading scientist that created the park's hybrid dinosaurs.

The film broke with the tradition of having CGI and animatronic dinosaurs side by side. Only the dying Apatosaurus' head was a real life creation by Legacy Effects, a company formed by former Stan Winston artists. All other dinosaurs were computer generated by ILM under supervision of *Jurassic Park* veteran Phill Tippett. Michael Giacchino returned to the *Jurassic Park* franchise as the film's composer. He created a new *Jurassic World* theme that was interweaved with John Williams' classic theme. The soundtrack was released both digitally and on CD.

The film was a commercial success, breaking several records and making it the highest grossing *Jurassic Park* franchise film upon its release in 2015.

Hasbro Toys

Hasbro once again produced the *Jurassic World* toys, but received some backlash over it. Many fans complained about the lack of action figures, the low quality of the plastic, sloppy paint jobs and visible screws. Despite all the backlash, toys like Mosasaurus, Ceratosaurus and Ankylosaurus were considered a good addition to the *Jurassic Park* toy universe. Hasbro announced in the summer of 2015 that its second-quarter net income rose thanks to the *Jurassic World* toy line.

There were several sublines: Bashers & Biters, Titans, Growlers, Versus and the big dinosaurs. The Bashers & Biters line were small dinosaurs with some basic actions, like moving heads or tails. Some of these dinosaurs were not in the film, like Spinosaurus,

Jurassic World Bashers & Biters: Tyrannosaurus Rex, Stegoceratops and Spinosaurus.

Jurassic World Bashers & Biters: Ankylosaurus, Pachycephalosaurus and Allosaurus.

Jurassic World Bashers & Biters: Stegoceratops repaint, Velociraptor 'Blue', Indominus Rex and Tyrannosaurus Rex repaint.

Allosaurus and Stegoceratops. The latter was a hybrid dinosaur, part Stegosaurus and part Triceratops. A concept drawing was referenced in the film on one of the computer screens in the lab. The Bashers & Biters were released in different waves. One of the

Jurassic World Velociraptor pack with exclusive 'Blue'.

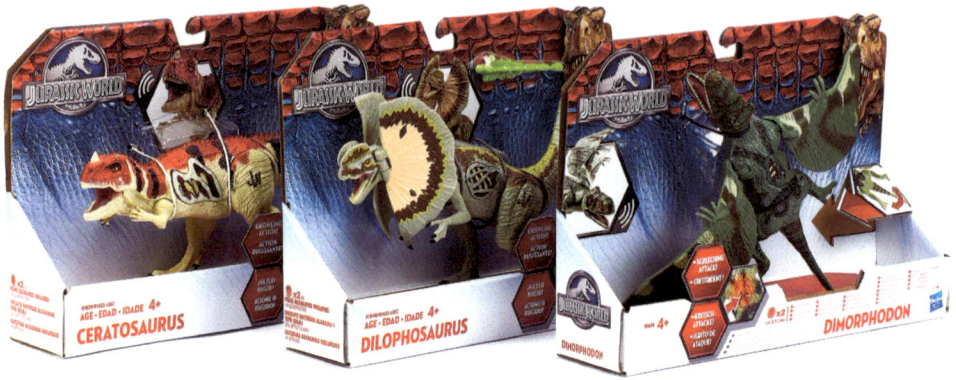

Jurassic World Growlers: Ceratosaurus, Dilophosaurus and Dimorphodon.

later waves included two repainted dinosaurs: the Tyrannosaurus Rex, in a bright green colour, and a Stegoceratops, in a tan colour.

The Titans were three Velociraptors – 'Charlie', 'Echo' and 'Delta' – which were each sold separately. These were quite controversial toys due to the lack of their iconic toe claw. A Target exclusive set combined all the Titan raptors and included a 'Blue' figure, which was exclusive for this set.

Seven dinosaurs were part of the Growlers subline. A dinosaur growl could be triggered by pushing the Dino-Damage wound, which also made the wound glow red.

The Dilophosaurus could launch a projectile from its mouth, mimicking its spitting action seen in the first film. A Dilophosaurus toy was produced for every *Jurassic Park* toy line that was inspired by a film.

The Versus line featured a creature and a vehicle with a small generic action figure. The dinosaurs in this line were the only ones with a Dino-Damage wound that could be healed. A little door could slide in front of the wound to cover it up. Although the entire toy line received some harsh reviews, it turned out that the Mosasaurus was one of the most popular in this toy line.

The Tyrannosaurus Rex Lockdown was inspired by the Raptor Attack Set from *Jurassic Park III*. Just like that set, it came with a large gate, several fences, a dinosaur and a net launcher. The set also came with a miniature gyrosphere with a printed cardboard figure inside instead of a real action figure. The Tyrannosaurus Rex was the same as the one from the Bashers & Biters line.

The Tyrannosaurus Rex with chomping jaws was one of the larger dinosaur toys. It had jaws that could mechanically open and close by pressing the button on its back. The sculpt was made entirely out of plastic and did not feature sound effects.

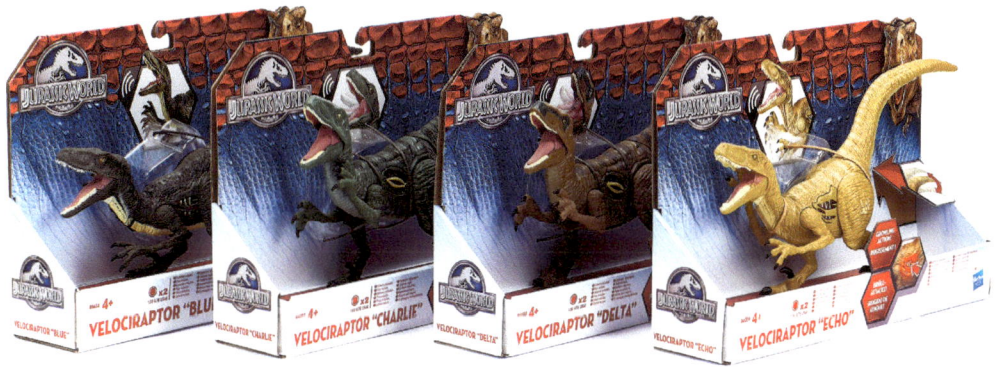

Jurassic World Growlers: 'Blue', 'Charlie', 'Delta', 'Echo'.

Jurassic World Pteranodon *v.* Helicopter and Indominus Rex *v.* Gyro Sphere.

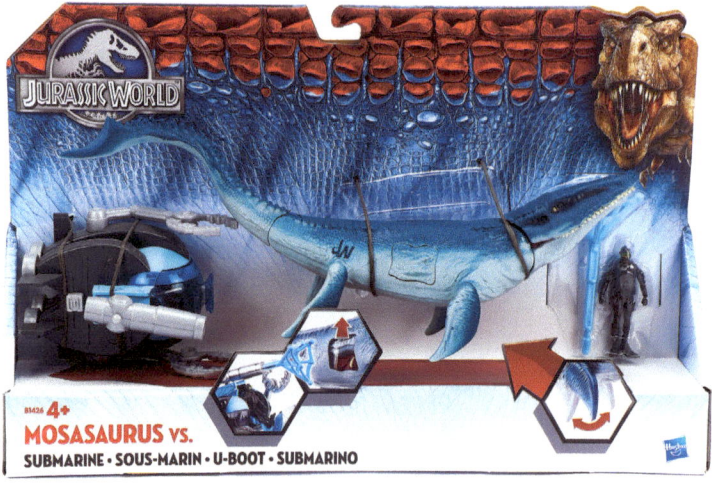

Jurassic World Mosasaurus *v.* Submarine.

Jurassic World Tyrannosaurus Rex Lockdown.

Jurassic World Tyrannosaurus Rex with chomping jaws.

The Electronic Stomp & Strike T-Rex was larger than the Chomping T-Rex and was a completely different sculpt. The body was much bulkier compared to the Chomping T-Rex. Sound effects could be triggered by pushing its tail down while standing on a surface. It would then raise its body, snap its jaws and produce a growl.

The largest dinosaur of this toy line was the Electronic Indominus Rex. Unlike the other dinosaurs, it featured a rubber-like skin, a reminder of the old Kenner dinosaurs. The Indominus Rex could growl and a light under its skin would light up.

Hasbro also used the *Jurassic World* license in their Hero Mashers toy line. All dinosaurs had removable body parts that could be swapped out for others so that new hybrids could be created.

The Playskool Heroes *Jurassic World* toy line was similar to the *Jurassic Park* Junior line, which was produced by Hasbro in 2001. It was designed with children between three and seven years in mind.

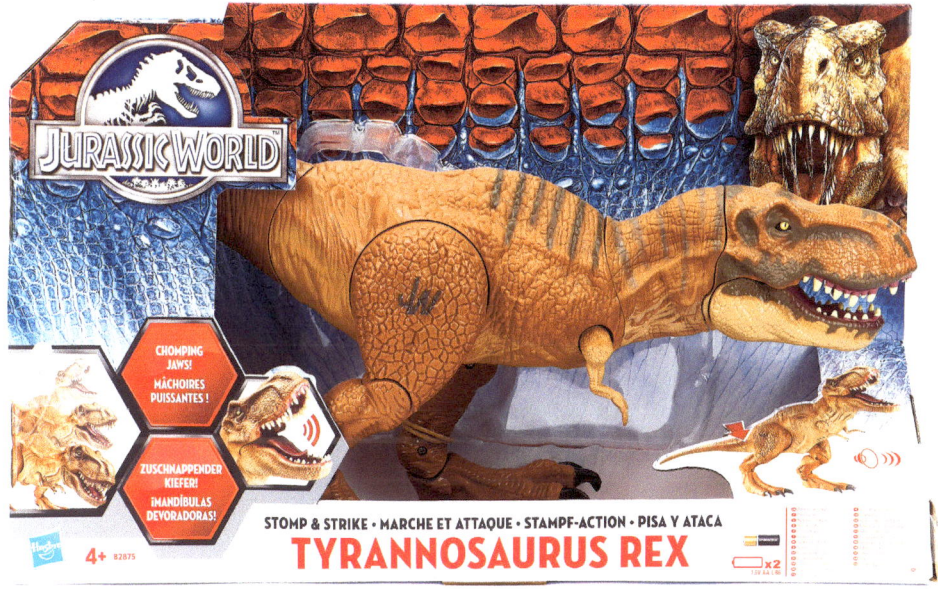

Above: Jurassic World Stomp & Strike Tyrannosaurus Rex.

Right: Jurassic World Indominus Rex.

A selection of *Jurassic World* Hero Mashers toys.

A selection of *Jurassic World* Playskool Heroes toys.

Other Toy Brands

LEGO produced six *Jurassic World* sets. All mini-figures that came with these sets were inspired by the film characters. Most of the dinosaur figures first appeared in the 2012 LEGO Dino line. The biggest set, with 1,156 LEGO pieces, was the Indominus Rex Breakout.

Traveller's Tales made a LEGO *Jurassic World* videogame that was based on all four *Jurassic Park* films. The game was single or multiplayer. A special edition was released with an exclusive Dr Wu mini-figure.

LEGO *Jurassic World* Pteranodon Capture, Dilophosaurus Ambush and Raptor Escape.

LEGO *Jurassic World* Raptor Rampage and T-Rex Tracker.

LEGO *Jurassic World* Indominus Rex Breakout.

LEGO *Jurassic World* videogame with exclusive Dr Wu mini-figure.

Remote-control Jeep Wrangler by Jada Toys.

Jurassic World Mission Force set by Matchbox.

Jada Toys acquired the *Jurassic World* license to produce die-cast vehicles that were featured in the film. Included in this line were a remote-controlled Jeep Wrangler and a Mercedes-Benz G 63 AMG 6x6. Jada also released several other *Jurassic World* vehicles in different scales.

Unlike Jada Toys, Mattel's Matchbox made a line of die-cast vehicles that were fantasy inspired. All kinds of land, air and water-based vehicles were part of this line. Each vehicle was sold separately, but some were combined in box sets.

Assorted *Jurassic World* Merchandising

Jurassic World miniature dinosaur blind bags by Hasbro.

Jurassic World plush by Hasbro.

Above left: *Jurassic World* Inflatable Tyrannosaurus Rex.

Above right: *Jurassic World* boxer shorts.

Below: *Jurassic World* excavation kits.

Jurassic World: Dino Hybrid

A Dino Hybrid line tried to follow the success of the first film's merchandise line. The concept was similar to *Jurassic Park:* Chaos Effect. Many of the hybrid creatures appeared in Ludio's *Jurassic World: The Game* for iOS and Android devices. Only a few suppliers went ahead with the license. Hasbro previewed their *Jurassic World:* Dino Hybrid toy line during the New York Toy Fair in 2016. All of Hasbro's hybrids used the original sculpts from the first line, but with different heads, paint jobs or added armour. The toys had a limited release, with only a few sets appearing outside the United States.

Hasbro Toys

Six small dinosaur hybrids were based on the Bashers & Biters dinosaurs from the first *Jurassic World* line: the Spinosaurus was a repaint and the Ankylosaurus and Indominus Rex came with a removable set of armour, while the Dilophosaurus Rex, Carnoraptor and Stegoceratops were modified sculpts.

Three Growler hybrids were part of this line. The Velociraptor and Dilophosaurus were repaints from the first line, but the Pteramimus was a completely new hybrid. It was based on the Dimorphodon sculpt but with a new head and wings.

The only action figure to be inspired by a character from the film was part of the Owen & Velociraptor set. Owen came with his motorcycle, as seen in the film, along with a re-issue of the 'Blue' figure from the Bashers & Biters line. An ultraviolet light could reveal a skin pattern on the raptor's back.

The Hybrid FX Tyrannosaurus Rex was based on the Chomping T-Rex, but this time with sound effects and spikes on its back, which could be raised by pushing a button.

Jurassic World Dino Hybrid Carnoraptor, Dilophosaurus Rex and Spinosaurus.

Jurassic World Dino Hybrid Armor Ankylosaurus, Armor Indominus Rex and Stegoceratops.

Jurassic World Dino Hybrid Velociraptor.

Jurassic World Dino Hybrid Pteramimus.

Jurassic World Dino Hybrid Dilophosaurus.

Jurassic World Dino Hybrid Owen 'Alpha' and Velociraptor 'Blue'.

Jurassic World Dino Hybrid FX Tyrannosaurus Rex.

Jurassic World Dino Hybrid Rampage Indominus Rex.

The biggest toy in this sequel toy line was the Hybrid Rampage Indominus Rex. It stood taller than the original Electronic Indominus Rex and no longer had a rubber-like skin. Red spikes were added to its back and an additional set of yellow spikes could be raised by pushing the button on its side. Pushing down its left arm triggered a mechanical chomping jaws effect.

Assorted *Jurassic World:* Dino Hybrid Merchandising

Jurassic World Dino Hybrid activity book.

Jurassic World (2015)

Jurassic World Dino Hybrid children's party set.

Jurassic World Dino Hybrid plush toys.

Ancient Future

It wasn't easy to compile a book about *Jurassic Park* collectibles. Hundreds of interesting items have been produced in the past twenty-five years, and many companies today continue that tradition by creating epic dinosaurs and memorable scenes from the *Jurassic Park* legacy. It was impossible to include every single collectible, but I hope I inspired you to start or expand your own *Jurassic Park* collection. Make it bigger, louder and with more teeth.

Acknowledgments

A loving thank you to my parents for all the time and effort they have put in helping me out with my collection. Thank you to Rob for his love, advice and patience while I was writing and editing. Thank you to my friends Francisco and Keith for all their help, even though we're almost 5,000 miles apart from each other. A shoutout to my *Jurassic Park* friends Dimitri and Alain. Alain runs the great website JPToys.com, which proved to be an excellent resource while researching the book. And, finally, thank you to all my social media followers, friends and work colleagues, who have advised, supported and encouraged me on this exciting trip to Isla Nublar and back.